Amor Vincit Omnia "Love Conquers All"

Ranjani Arul

BookLeaf Publishing

India | USA | UK

Presentation by *BookLeaf Publishing*

Web: www.bookleafpub.com

E-mail: info@bookleafpub.com

ISBN: 9789358313369

First edition 2024

DEDICATION

My life itself is dedicated to the man

Who raised me like a

"Princess"

This book is dedicated to the "King"

who saw the "Queen" in me

"In the world full of people with fake Love;

You and I are Icon of True Love"

"The Queen is waiting.

Waiting for her king

King needs to be there.

There, where they're both next to each other in
the bed

In bed, where it feels like heaven

Like in heaven, when the king breathes

Breathing next to her so close

so close that the queen captures his soul.

His soul, where everything belongs

Belongings of him became her's.

Her whole body and soul became his own.

Owning the Queen like he owns the empire."

ACKNOWLEDGEMENT

Whom should i thank
To be frank
Thanking the one above all
He will play with our destiny like a football
Thanking who gave me life
You both made me alive
Thanking the one born with me
That's why "I" became "we"
Thanking everyone in my family
Grateful to have a family like this, thank fully
Thanking the one who inspired me to write
Because of you everything feels so right
Thanking the beautiful soul who's reading this
Let me give you a virtual kiss
Thanking the nature for being so nice
You opened my eyes
Thanking "love"
Because winning over you is so tough
Let's give limitless love to everyone
Without expecting any outcome

PREFACE

What should i say
Should i write an essay
Writing this feels like a dream
Because it's love themed
Am i in love ?
I'm dedicating this to my beloved
Writing this for him
In my heart, I found you within
I've met you with zero expectation
Without any preparation
What should i say if they ask me about you
Should i say , you're my best view
You came in to my life out of blue
You're making me go crazy
Can I expect something other than your maybe
Say yes, because I Wanna be your only lady

Idyllic

Whenever I feel low,
You somehow make me glow.
Let me take it slow.
I want to go with the flow.
Whenever you talk to me, though
My heart feels like a dessert filled with snow.
What kinda feeling is this? I still don't know.
Suddenly, love came in and waved a sweet hello.
I didn't say No.
Even though sometimes I don't know
How to show
Since I'm not a pro
But I know. You know.
Together with love, we grow.

Longing

When I look at the pretty blue sky,
I remember your smile.
When I hear those calm beach waves,
I remember your breath.
When I look at the beautiful moon,
I remember your shining eyes.
Why are you making me waiting?
Can't you see that I'm melting?
You keep testing, and I'm crying.
The longing for you is never-ending.
The distance between us is killing.
You're the only one for me.
I'm all down on my knees.
All I want to do right now,
is to feel you in my arms.
All I want to do right now,
is to see you, my man.

Obsession

What I see in you is something that can't be
explained.
Every time I hear your voice, I get excited.
Is this a coincidence or God's plan?
You made me go like, "Wow, what a man!"
You took my heart effortlessly.
You made me yours ruthlessly.
Every time I hear your name, I go numb.
Seriously? those things you magically made me do
for you!Ain't no fun.
How could I trust a man this much?
I used to think that there's nothing like "love" as
such.

You changed me for the better.
My life has become sweeter.
I'm doing everything.
And anything
Only for you, Wow!
I don't know how
Finally, I put my crown facedown.
Well, you made me bow down.

Valued

When people said, I Can't
You said, I can
When they laughed at my dream,
You were on my team.
When they ignored me
You gave me your love for free.
When they bullied my song
You asked me to stay strong.
When they left me
You were my trustee.
Thank you so much for being there.
When I can't go anywhere
You are my best friend.
Please be with me until "the very end."

Ecstasy

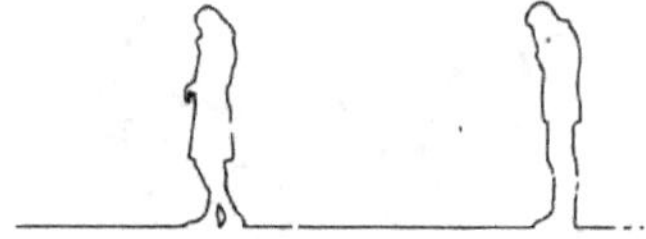

I wish there's no distance in between.
Please, come and get your queen.
I wish we are together right now.
So, I could feel your heartbeat right now.
Whenever you hug me so tight with your gleaming skin
It makes me feel like someone is playing violin.
The moment I feel you inside me
I'll gulp for a second before I scream.
My skin will burn from the happiness you gave
I'll be your forever slave.
We both embrace each other like lotus flower.
Together, we become superpower.

Yearning

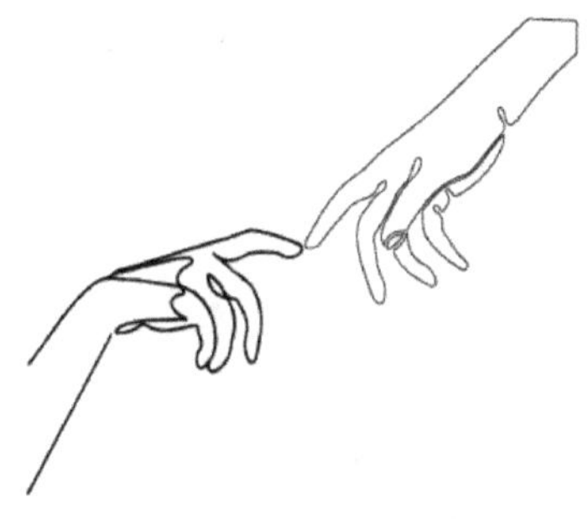

Why do I miss you so much?
All I want right now is to feel your touch.
My heart keeps aching.
I keep praying.
Your touch will be my only medicine.
which is needed in a dozen!
You take my heart to the land of peace.
For that, I want you to be here.
And I want you to touch me everywhere.
which will take my oxytocin somewhere.
When will you let me inside you
Wherever I go, all I see is you.
Seeing your face keeps me alive.
I want you in my life to survive.
No one ever made me feel this way.
I used to tell everyone to "stay away."

You're shining so bright.
Is it possible to keep this moon only to my eyesight?
I don't want to share my moon with anyone.
I became so selfish, I don't know how to overcome
Waiting to see my king's beautiful smile
Your queen is the only one who has acquired those
rights.

Oneness

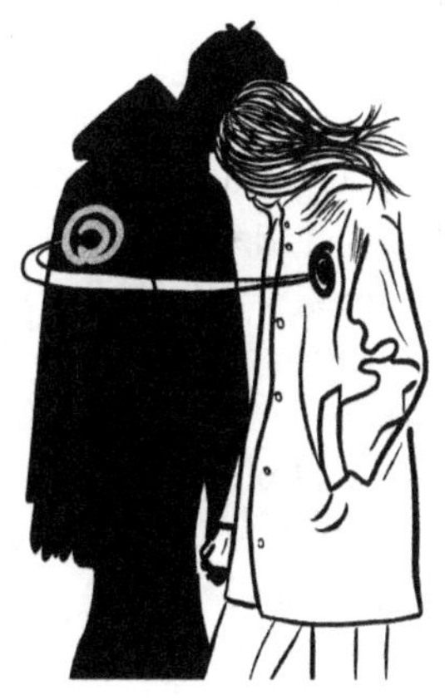

Why would I be angry at you?
For you being you
That's why I fell for you.
Among these million people
You're the only one who makes me feel so peaceful.
That is why our love became powerful.
Never apologize. You're enough and wonderful.
We don't need to talk all the time.
You're my soul's rhyme.
I'm inside your heart everywhere.
And I can feel your presence anywhere.
Think about me for once.
I hope, smile comes.
I don't want to put you under pressure.

But allow me to be in your heart forever.
The truth is, that's where I want to be.
Please say yes and agree.
Let me in there.
Lock me in there.
Allow me to own you.
My love for you is so true.
Even if you can't reach out to me physically,
Still, I could feel your breath magically.
Because I'm always inside you.
You're inside me too.
Now, we both have each other.
Let's become lovers.
There's nothing to control.
As soon as we become a whole
We're two bodies, one soul.

Unique

Remembering the day I came to know you
A very few can be like you.
Knowing you feels like a mystery.
You took my heart to love victory.
Very few made me feel like this.
Every nerve of mine wants you to be my first kiss.
Completely captivated by your pure soul.
Mercilessly, you took my heart as a whole.
I initially thought this was another joke.
Now, I'm damn sure this feeling isn't a joke.
I was researching how God might have made you.
Amused by the way, he made you
Beautiful people are not real, they say.
Honestly, you have to say
"The universe broke this law for me to convey
People like me do exist.
You can't resist."

Rhapsody

I was lost in my life.
I want to kill myself with a knife.
You came into my life.
Because of you, I've survived.
God sent you to be mine.
You're so pure, like divine.
Nothing can be more perfect.
I've got so much respect.
If I could do anything,
I'll pray for you to have everything
Am I lucky enough to keep you?
Because you're so true.
You're so full of goodness.
You take away everyone's sadness.
People like "You" do exist

Till now, I've missed
Where were you for this long?
Now, you have become my favorite song.
Thank you for coming into my life.
You made me feel alive.
You're my forever loop song.
I've waited for you so long.

Urge

Why do I want you all the time?
You always commit this crime.
You're making me wait for so long.
But still, I'm staying strong.
Everywhere I go, I see you.
I want you to be my only view.
I want you so close.
All of your scars, I want to know
I want you to embrace me so tight.
That's the only thing that makes me feel so right.
I lay my face on your chest.
Those are the moments, I want to invest.
Touch my heart, touch my body.
Only you have those rights; else nobody.

Passion

We keep wanting each other.
While the distance makes us suffer,
I'm waiting for the day when you can touch me
anywhere.
The surroundings won't be a nightmare.
You take a step closer.
We don't need to take things slower.
We watch our clothes fall off slowly.
The moment our eyes get locked, it's going to be
holy.
From head to toe, let's do something unholy.
It's going to be the moment we feel so true, mostly
The burning in our bodies when we look
The moment of silence we took
to reach the places we wanted
The heat waves are getting started.

You embrace me with your whole body.
I no longer be someone's somebody.
We became one.
Finally, we won.

Idolize

Trust me, my king, I breathe for you.
It feels like I have the flu.
You have no clue.
In my head, I did so many reviews.
Still, my love for you grew.
Because you're so true.
I feel like a raindrop in mountain dew.
I want to sink into your skin like your tattoo.
Even the little moments with you, I want to redo
This feeling I have for you, I won't undo.
Let me say a million "thank you."
for being trustworthy among the very few
I could stand in the queue.
To get you as my forever view
This feels so new.
You're the only one. This queen wants to be with
you.

Nonpareil

You're like the moon in my night.
You're glimmering so bright.
Without you, my sky feels empty.
The land of mine becomes unhealthy.
I can only look at you from far away.
Catching you is impossible; I can only pray.
Will I ever get to catch you?
Everybody wants a piece of you.
Having you in my sky is enough.
Is it really enough?
There is so much going on in my life.
Still, thoughts about you make my soul revive.
Your smile brightens my day.
Are you a god or a magician? Please say
When my eyes kiss yours
All of my lustful thoughts cure
Describing your beauty in words is hard.
You must be a Greek God.

Destiny

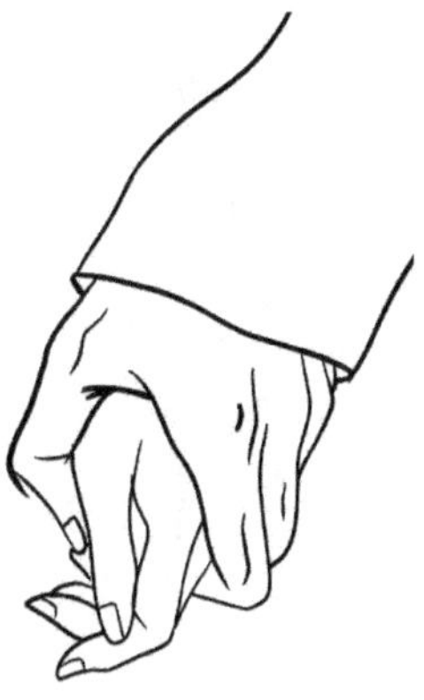

I would never, ever hate you.
You're one of the precious few.
Why would I hate the man I love?
Even though he's rough and tough,
Thank you for letting me into your life.
Is it wrong? If I say I want to be your wife,
I don't have enough courage to say
I just don't know any other way.
Writing this book to convey
That's the only way.
I'm afraid to express myself. What if I lose you?
Because of what I have gone through
I hope you understand me.
Also, I don't want you to hate me.
What you read was right.

Don't hide in plain sight.
I'll take every bad thing coming your way.
I just hope you want me to stay.
Life has been hard.
We have been through a lot.
Let's face it together.
Say the word "forever."
Only if you're okay
Otherwise, I'll make my way.
Please ask me to stay.

Expressive

I wonder, what's on your mind?
I want to see everything behind.
Your eyes, wish I could read.
All of those words unsaid.
Tell me your secrets.
I will keep it private.
I'll keep everything in a safer place.
It only opens when we embrace
each other, what's behind
Those eyes are one of a kind.
Every time I look at you,
I can feel through
There are a million words unspoken.
In this connection,
We don't need to say anything.
The sound of our hearts says everything.

Do we need words to express?
I don't want you to confess.
Even from your silence
I can still complete your sentence.
Love needs no words.
That's the truth of this whole world.
Finally, women with expressive words.
Got, man with beautiful thoughts but few words.

Radiant

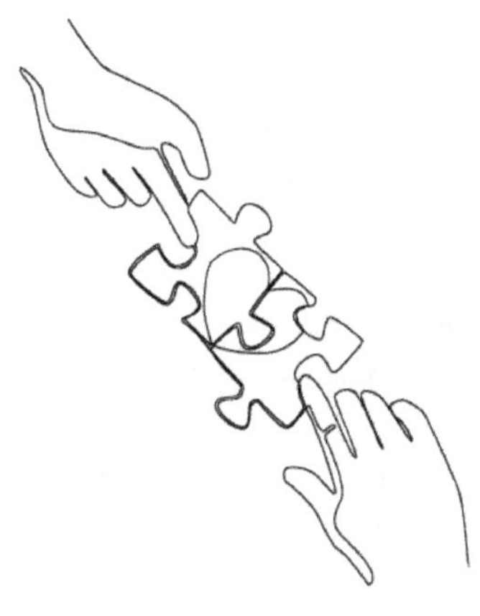

You're always right.
The one who wants me to shine bright
The way you care about me is so real.
You're the one who's making me heal.
Sometimes I do think too much.
It becomes so much.
Every single stuff
Indeed, I make it so tough.
I make the same mistakes.
Still, you never let me shake.
Why are you being so kind?
You're the best man on mankind
I don't understand how someone can be this
beautiful.
Even though I act so juvenile,
They say no one can forgive you too much.
There won't be a man nonesuch.

You're too much to handle.
You won't be getting loved even a little.
Who will tolerate you?
Anyhow, you're going to screw
Just like Lord Rama broke the bow
You made these people say, Wow.
You're treating me so well.
You're making me come through out of hell.
They said, Stop being a princess.
No one is going to treat you with the kindness
You came and broke everything they said.
Leaving me behind instead
You stood beside me with a high head.
Still walking with me on the road ahead
Thank you won't be enough.
You're my beloved.
No one else is above.
Give me a chance to repay you.
But how? I have no clue.
All I can do is pray to God.
To remove all the odd
I wish to be the rose under your feet.
While you walk on the street
So no one will mistreat
Even if it's your feet.

Stardust

I was about to die.
I wanted to say goodbye.
You came into my life.
Because of you, I've survived.
You're one of a kind.
Your love is much needed in mankind.
My wings were broken.
Wounds were unspoken.
You came and healed.
and became my shield.
You wanted me to fly.
I gave it a try.
You took my hand.
made me understand
I don't need wings to fly high.

Whatever happens, I should standby.
You said, I have the Lord's heart.
I'm his handmade art.
You're my missing piece.
Oh! My darling, you're God's ultimate masterpiece.

Inseparable

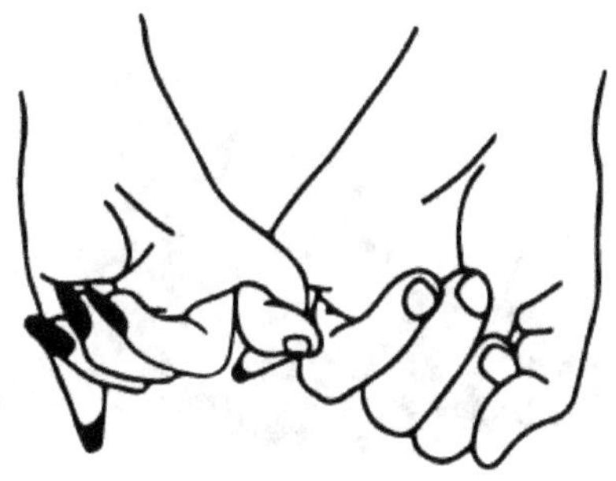

I don't want to talk about your past.
Life is so fast.
I just want to think less.
It won't make us feel stressed.
Let's live in this moment together.
Until all the things we want will gather
We will talk about "forever."
Trust me, I'll be here.
I'm so in love with you, my dear. Are you clear?
If I say that, I won't be leaving.
Trust me, you're not dreaming.
Holding hands forever
It means I completely surrender.
I'll take care of you.
That's so true.

Night Sky

A day when I wanted sunlight
You came into my life as moonlight.
Always worried about getting lost somewhere
You took my hope elsewhere.
Receiving someone like you from God was like a
boon.
You helped me shine in the night like a moon.
Rarest gem like you were found nowhere.
Without you, my life would have been a nightmare.
Entering a cave without a light
Having you in my life just feels so right.
Thank you won't be enough.
Without you, my life would have been tough.
On this planet, no one can be as kind as you.
There will be people like you; I never knew
You make me feel so special.
How come you're so gentle?
In your arms, I feel safe.

Please be my better half.
Blessed to have a man like you
In this world, gems like you are very few.

Gleaming

You made me think, Where have you been before?
Your love is the only thing I crave more.
Nothing is bad; after all, we're humans.
Together, we can find solutions.
We're not here to drift apart.
We knew it from the very start.
We met because we deserved each other.
Even though it will go to a point where it will be
tougher
Facing each other's evilness is no big deal.
In this connection, we don't conceal
Girls will leave you.
Women like me will stick to you like glue.
If you know how to be good and bad at the same
time,
You're committing no crime.
Maybe the world will misunderstand.

but I kinda understand
To Err is human.
That's why you're my superhuman.
People try to become God.
I find it very odd.
We live in a place where we make mistakes.
And learn from every heartbreak.
Everybody got some lightness and darkness.
That's what makes us so US.
Please be you.
You're my best view.

Heart strong

All of my life, I have been searching for a melody.
Then you came into my life as a remedy.
Your voice is still echoing in my head.
Until I sleep in my bed
Always, it feels like I've known you for years.
When I see you, all of my sorrow disappears.
I reach out my hand for your touch.
I don't know why I want it so much.
I never liked anyone in my life.
As much as I wanted to be your wife,
I've lived my life like a monk.
You came into my life; it feels like I'm drunk.
I swear to God.
This feeling is so hot.
Sometimes I even wonder
Why do I need to surrender?

Your love keeps me awake.
but still, I don't want to take a break.
I wrote a million poems without emotion.
But for you, I feel devotion.
My love for you is deep, like an ocean.
because you're the one, God-chosen
I thought of writing you this.
This time I don't want to miss
until I get my very first kiss!

9 789358 313369